MAZES
THROUGH
TIME

45 Thrilling Mazes Packed
with Facts About the Past →

Art by Marc Pattenden
Words by Matt Yeo

ARCTURUS

ARCTURUS

This edition published in 2022 by Arcturus Publishing Limited
26/27 Bickels Yard, 151–153 Bermondsey Street,
London SE1 3HA

Author: Matt Yeo
Illustrator: Marc Pattenden
Designer: Mark Golden
Editor: Violet Peto
Packaged by Cloud King Creative
Consultant: Ian Fitzgerald
Design Manager: Jessica Holliland
Managing Editor: Joe Harris

ISBN: 978-1-3988-2019-7
CH010110NT
Supplier 42, Date 0922, PI 00001957

Printed in Singapore

CONTENTS

EARLY HUMANS

We don't know very much about the lives of primitive humans. The period before the written word is called prehistory.

Many new species emerged after the extinction of the dinosaurs. These included all sorts of mammals, plants, and marine life.

HELP GUIDE *HOMO ERECTUS* BACK TO THE SAFETY OF HIS CAVE DWELLING!

START

Homo habilis lived on Earth more than 2 million years ago. They are believed to have been the first humans to use basic tools.

Emerging more than
2 million years ago,
Homo erectus is thought
to be the first species
to use fire to cook
their food.

FINISH

Early hominids learned
to seek shelter from
the elements and
predators in caves,
and they learned to
make their own tents
and huts.

5

THE STONE AGE

One of the longest periods in human history, the Stone Age lasted roughly 3.4 million years and ended around 2000 BCE.

WHICH PATH SHOULD THE NEANDERTHAL MAN TAKE TO REACH THE REST OF HIS TRIBE!

START

It was during the Stone Age that primitive dogs became domesticated. They helped humans hunt and would have made good pets!

Neanderthals looked very similar to modern humans, but they were heavier and more muscular, with long faces and wide noses.

FINISH

Most early hominid species eventually died out, but some evolved into modern humans, now known as *Homo sapiens*.

At the start of the Stone Age, humans hunted animals and gathered fruit and nuts. By the end of it they had learned how to grow their own crops.

7

THE FIRST CITIES

Between 10,000 and 4000 BCE, early human settlements began to grow in size and eventually evolved into the first cities.

Mesopotamia was the birthplace of one of the first civilizations.

START

FOLLOW THE WINDING PATH THROUGH THE DESERT TO REACH THE ANCIENT CITY OF SUMER!

One of the most important inventions in the history of the world is the wheel, which was first built by the Sumerians!

The Sumerians were the first civilization to develop writing. They used over 500 pictographs, which evolved into words.

The city of Sumer was in the southern part of Mesopotamia. The Sumerians built huge temples known as ziggurats.

FINISH

FAMOUS PHARAOHS

The rise of the pharaohs began in Egypt over 5,000 years ago with King Menes. In the centuries to come, the pharaohs would build gigantic pyramids.

START

HELP THE SLAVE ESCAPE FROM THE EGYPTIAN GUARDS AND REACH THE SAFETY OF THE RIVER NILE!

Egyptians used pictures and symbols to write. This unique collection of characters is known as hieroglyphics.

The Great Pyramid of Giza is the oldest of the Seven Wonders of the World. It was 147 m (481.4 ft) tall when completed.

The Great Sphinx was built during the reign of King Khafre. At 20 m (66 ft) tall, it has the head of a pharaoh and the body of a lion!

At a length of over 6,650 km (4,132 mi), the River Nile was an important resource for ancient Egyptians.

FINISH

WALK LIKE AN EGYPTIAN

Ancient Egyptians believed that when a person died, they passed on to the afterlife.

Anubis was the Egyptian god of the dead who guarded the gates to the underworld. He had the head of a jackal.

Bodies were wrapped in bandages to preserve or mummify them. The Egyptians even mummified their cats!

FIND THE RIGHT PATH OUT OF THE PYRAMID OR YOU MIGHT END UP STUCK INSIDE WITH THE MUMMIES!

START

It's believed that the ancient Egyptians aligned the pyramids with two stars: Kochab and Mizar (aka The Indestructibles).

Papyrus was a kind of paper that the Egyptians used for writing. It was made from the insides of the stems of the papyrus plants that grew along the River Nile.

FINISH

GETTING PHILOSOPHICAL

Ancient Greece was one of the most advanced civilizations in the world between 700 BCE and 480 BCE.

WHICH PATH SHOULD THE GREEK STUDENT TAKE THROUGH THE ACROPOLIS TO REACH THE PHILOSOPHERS?

START

During this period, architecture and philosophy flourished in ancient Greece. The Olympic Games also began there in 776 BCE.

Archimedes was a Greek with many talents. He was an inventor, scientist, mathematician, and astronomer!

The temples and statues of the Acropolis in Athens were built during the city's golden age. They were constructed in worship of the Greek goddess, Athena.

Pythagoras, Aristotle, and Plato all studied philosophy to learn more about the world around them.

FINISH

MYTHS AND LEGENDS

Ancient Greece is famous for its rich mythology. The Greeks created many incredible stories about gods, heroes, and monsters.

In one myth, a prince called Theseus had to enter a labyrinth and battle a bull-headed monster called the Minotaur!

It's said that anyone who looked into the eyes of Medusa would turn to stone. She was defeated by the hero, Perseus.

START

GUIDE THE SPARTAN WARRIOR THROUGH THE TWISTING MAZE TO REACH THE STATUE IN THE MIDDLE.

Sparta was ruled by two kings of the Agiad and Eurypontid families, both of which claimed to be descended from Heracles!

The most powerful of the gods was Zeus. The ancient Greeks believed he caused thunderstorms when he was angry.

FINISH

RIVERS OF BABYLON

The Babylonian Empire was a state in Mesopotamia famous for its legendary Hanging Gardens.

The Hanging Gardens were one of the Seven Wonders of World. They were built by King Nebuchadnezzar II in around 600 BCE.

LEAD THE QUEEN THROUGH THE HANGING GARDENS TO REACH HER HUSBAND, THE KING.

START

The King built the Hanging Gardens for his wife, Amytis, who missed the forests and meadows of her homeland.

FINISH

Babylon means "Gate of God." The Hanging Gardens are considered by some to be a myth, as only a few ruins have been found.

The Hanging Gardens were believed to be more than 22.86 m (75 ft) high, and the plants tumbled down over the pyramid-shaped structure.

THE GREAT WALL

Qin Shi Huang, the first emperor of China, ordered construction of the first wall in the third century BCE as protection from enemy attacks.

During the Ming Dynasty in the mid-1500s, major repairs were made to the Great Wall. Some sections that were built with earth were replaced with bricks.

Over 7,000 lookout watchtowers were built along the Great Wall. If soldiers spotted an attack, they would use smoke signals as a warning.

START

HELP GUIDE THE BUILDER THROUGH THE WINDING MAZE TO DELIVER BRICKS TO COMPLETE THE WALL!

Completed in 1878, the wall is 4–8m (13–26ft) wide and 5–8m (16–26ft) high!

There have been many battles at the Great Wall, including a fight between the Empire of Japan and the Republic of China in 1933.

FINISH

CHINESE INVENTIONS

Some of the greatest inventions and scientific discoveries of all time originated thousands of years ago in China.

Paper and printing were invented in China in around 100 CE. Paper was made using hemp and other plant materials.

CAN YOU LEAD THE GUARD THROUGH THE NARROW STREETS TO REACH THE AMAZING FIREWORK DISPLAY?

START

The first primitive lodestone compasses were being used by the Chinese during the second century BCE.

Fireworks were invented more than 2,000 years ago. Some villagers used them to scare off "mountain men!"

FINISH

The Chinese first used gunpowder as far back as the Tang Dynasty (618–907 CE). Incendiary bombs were launched from catapults.

RACE TO SURVIVE

A popular sport in both ancient Greece and Rome, chariot racing was entertaining for crowds, but very dangerous for drivers and horses.

Chariots had two wheels and were pulled by up to four horses. Drivers could use weapons to attack other charioteers.

START

RACE AROUND THE TRACK IN YOUR CHARIOT AND SEE IF YOU CAN MAKE IT TO THE FINISH LINE IN ONE PIECE!

Fearless charioteers were often slaves who raced to gain their freedom. One of the most famous was Diocles, who raced for 24 years!

The very best races were
held in the Circus Maximus
in the city of Rome. Men,
women, children, and even
emperors all went to watch!

FINISH

During the rule of the Roman
Empire, special racetracks called
circuses were built for people
to view the sport.

ROMAN CONQUEST

At one point in its history, the Roman Empire included Britain, Spain, Egypt, Greece, and many other countries.

HELP THE CENTURION MAKE HIS WAY ACROSS THE WESTERN PART OF THE VAST ROMAN EMPIRE.

START

Once they conquered a country, the Romans began building roads, bridges, aqueducts, and walls.

The Roman army was said to be so strong that they could march up to 40 km (24.8 mi) a day and still fight!

The Roman Empire was so vast that it was divided into provinces, each ruled by a governor. They in turn reported to the emperor.

In 27 BCE Caesar Augustus became the first Roman emperor. The month of August is named after him!

FINISH

THE PERSIAN EMPIRE

Stretching from Turkey and Egypt across to the north of India and Central Asia, the Persian Empire lasted from around 550 BCE–330 BCE.

Cyrus the Great led a large group of different tribes and together they managed to conquer the Babylonians.

A later ruler, Darius the Great, had a massive royal road network built for him that was over 12,874 km (8,000 mi) long!

GUIDE THE PERSIAN ARCHER THROUGH THE BATTLE TO REACH THE REST OF HIS ARMY!

START

Xerxes the Great was the son of Darius and fought in the Battle of Thermopylae and the Battle of Salamis.

FINISH

The Persians were defeated by the Greek army at the Battle of Marathon, eventually leading to the end of the empire.

INCREDIBLE INDIA

From its rise as an ancient civilization to its golden age under the Gupta Dynasty and the later rule of the Rajputs, India has a rich history.

The Gupta Dynasty lasted from around 320–550 CE and saw many achievements in the arts, science, and religion.

Ancient India established some of the first universities in the world. Nalanda in Bihar was one of the greatest.

SEE IF YOU CAN WORK OUT THE CORRECT PATH TO MAKE IT THROUGH THE TRICKY TAJ MAHAL MAZE!

START

Also known as the "crown of palaces," the Taj Mahal was built between 1632–1648 and is 73 m (240 ft) tall!

The Rajputs were descended from Hindu warriors and ruled the princely states of Rajasthan and Surashtra until the twentieth century.

FINISH

ALEXANDER THE GREAT

One of the greatest warriors and rulers of all time, Alexander the Great was born in Pella, Macedonia in 356 BCE.

MAKE YOUR WAY THROUGH THE EPIC BATTLE TO REACH ALEXANDER THE GREAT AT THE END OF THE MAZE!

START

Alexander the Great was said to be related to the legendary Greek heroes Heracles and Achilles.

By the age of 30, Alexander had conquered much of Europe, the Persian Empire, and India. He never lost a single battle!

One of Alexander's
tutors was the famous
Greek philosopher,
Aristotle, who taught
him science, politics,
and drama.

Alexander rode a
mighty steed called
Bucephalus into battle.
Stories say only
Alexander was able to
tame the horse!

FINISH

THE MAYA

An advanced society, the Maya people lived in Mesoamerica, where modern day Mexico and Central America is located.

The Maya people were extremely clever and invented their own calendars, farming methods, writing, sports, and religion.

Maya culture flourished from 1000 BCE through to 1697 CE. There were many Maya kings constantly at war with each other.

CAN YOU LEAD THE JAGUAR THROUGH THE MAZE AS IT WINDS ITS WAY THROUGH THE ANCIENT TEMPLE!

START

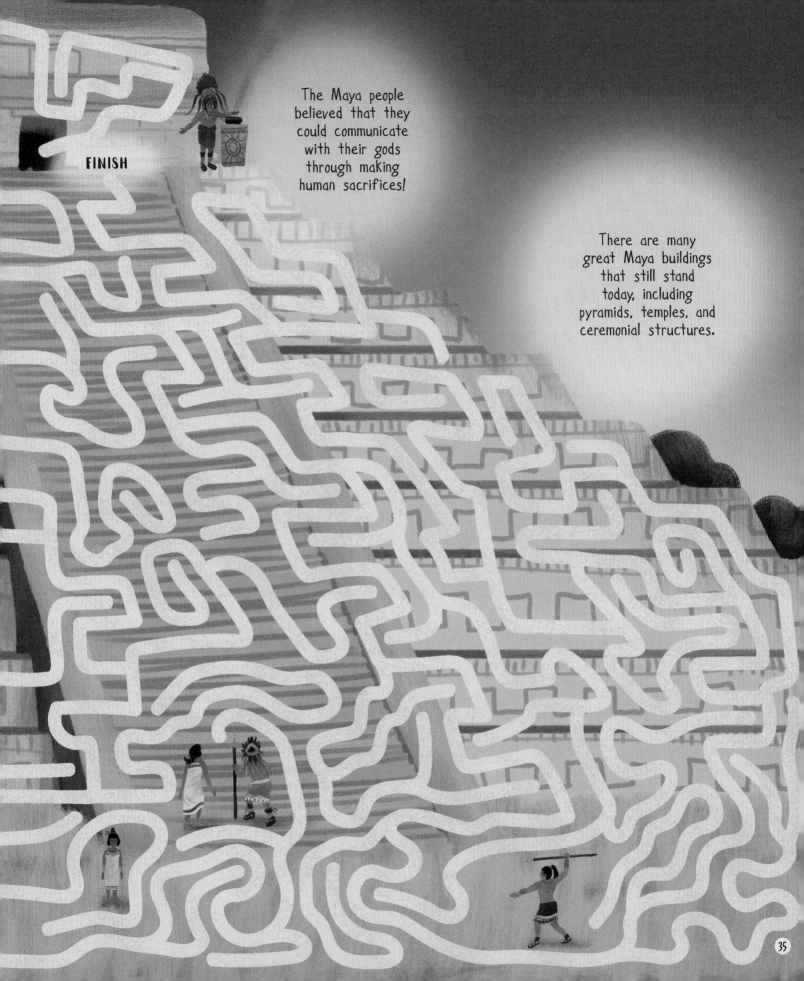

DEFENDING THE ROMAN EMPIRE

The sprawling Roman Empire had many enemies and used various techniques to keep the barbarian threat at bay, including a wall in Britain.

GUIDE THE ROMAN CENTURION OVER HADRIAN'S WALL TO STOP THE CELTS FROM ATTACKING!

START

In Britain, the Romans built Hadrian's Wall to defend the northwestern frontier of the province from invaders. It stretched 118 km (73 mi).

Eventually, invasions by the Goths, Franks, Huns, and weak emperors meant the Romans could no longer hold on to power.

At every Roman mile along the wall there was a small fort topped with a tower. Up to 30 soldiers could be stationed inside. There were also 17 large forts.

FINISH

The Roman Empire finally succumbed to the "barbarian" threat in 476 CE, falling to the Germanic leader, Odoacer.

CONSTANTINE THE GREAT

One of the greatest Roman emperors, Constantine, ruled from 306-337 CE and helped reunite a fractured empire.

After conquering Rome, Constantine decided to become a Christian and made laws to ensure they would not be persecuted.

When the previous emperor died in 306 CE, Constantine fought in a civil war to ultimately take control of Rome.

MAKE YOUR WAY THROUGH THE STREETS OF ROME TO VIEW THE STATUE OF CONSTANTINE!

START

In 330 CE, Constantine created a new Roman capital at the site of the ancient city of Byzantium, calling it Constantinople.

Constantine ruled the empire until his death in 337 CE. He was buried in the Church of the Holy Apostles in Constantinople.

FINISH

THE VIKINGS

Hailing from Scandinavia, the Viking people lived from around the late eighth to eleventh centuries. They were a fierce warrior race!

FOLLOW THE VIKINGS THROUGH THE FJORD AND OVER THE MOUNTAINS TO JOIN THEM ON THEIR NEXT CONQUEST.

START

There were many gods revered by the Vikings including Thor the god of thunder and his father, the wise Odin.

The Vikings called themselves "Ostmen" and built incredible longboats with which they sailed to other lands and conquered them.

When a Viking
warrior died, his body
was placed on a boat,
which was set on
fire and pushed out
into water!

The Vikings attacked
Britain many times,
battling the Anglo-Saxons
and establishing a large
kingdom around York.

THE ISLAMIC EMPIRE

The Islamic Golden Age, from the eighth to the fourteenth centuries, was a time of prosperity and scientific advancement.

The vast Islamic Empire stretched from northern Africa and Spain to as far away as parts of Asia and India.

During the Islamic Golden Age, the Abbasid Caliphate ruled from 750–1258 CE.

EXPLORE THE BUSTLING BAGHDAD MARKET AND MAKE YOUR WAY THROUGH IT TO THE EXIT!

START

The Islamic Golden Age came to an end when the much-feared Mongol warriors attacked Baghdad in 1258 CE.

The cultural hub of the Islamic Empire was the capital of Baghdad. It was home to artists, teachers, and scientists.

FINISH

THE CRUSADES

A series of supposedly holy wars in which Christian Europeans strove to "free" Jerusalem from Muslims, the Crusades lasted over 200 years.

The battle cry of the Crusaders from a speech by the Pope was "Deus vult!" which translates as "God wills it."

QUICKLY GUIDE THE KNIGHT THROUGH THE RAGING DESERT BATTLE TO REACH RICHARD I AT HIS CAMP!

START

Saladin was a famous Muslim leader during the Crusades. His greatest success was the recapture of Jerusalem in 1187 CE.

King Richard I, also known as "Richard the Lionheart," joined the Third Crusade for 10 months in 1191 CE.

FINISH

There were nine Crusades in total. Christians managed to capture Jerusalem in the First Crusade but lost it later.

THE AZTECS AND INCAS

Two dominant and advanced civilizations emerged in Mexico and South America in the 1400s—the Aztecs and Incas.

The capital city of the Aztec Empire was Tenochtitlan. It was planned out like a grid, with the king's palace at its heart.

HELP THE MESSENGER FIND HIS WAY THROUGH THE INCA CITY TO REACH THE KING AND DELIVER HIS NEWS.

START

The Aztecs built large temple pyramids and fought with other tribes to capture people to sacrifice to their gods!

The Inca ruled over the west coast of South America, until conquered by the Spanish conquistadors in 1532.

FINISH

The Inca had a complex government and system of roads, as well as a society where everyone had a job, home, and food.

THE MONGOL EMPIRE

Lasting from the thirteenth to fourteenth century, the Mongol Empire was one of the largest in history.

The empire was ruled by the great Mongol Khans and was founded by Genghis Khan in 1206 CE.

Genghis Khan was a very successful warrior and leader. He united the Mongol tribes and conquered much of China.

START

GUIDE GENGHIS KHAN AND HIS MONGOL ARMY THROUGH THE WINDING MOUNTAIN PASS.

The Mongol empire was vast and at its height included Eastern Europe, Central and Western Asia, and the Middle East.

Genghis Khan's grandson, Kublai Khan, would also go on to be a great leader and establish the Yuan Dynasty.

FINISH

THE RENAISSANCE

As Europe started to emerge from the Dark Ages, it entered a period of great cultural rebirth.

EXPLORE THE WORKS OF ART IN LEONARDO DA VINCI'S STUDIO AS HE CREATES HIS NEXT MASTERPIECE!

START

The era was known as the Renaissance and was a time of education, art, science, literature, music, and better living.

Leonardo da Vinci sketched many different designs for flying machines, including this one with a rotating propeller.

The Renaissance began
in Florence, Italy.
Venice was famous for
its glass work and
Milan was known for
its ironwork.

Leonardo da Vinci
was a master painter,
sculptor, scientist,
inventor, architect,
engineer, and writer.

FINISH

AGE OF EXPLORATION

From the late fifteenth century, European explorers began to map out the world and discover new lands.

NAVIGATE THE SHIP THROUGH UNCHARTED WATERS TO REACH A STRANGE NEW CONTINENT.

START

In 1620, a ship called the *Mayflower* transported the Pilgrim Fathers from England to North America.

Christopher Columbus was a famous Italian explorer who sailed to the Caribbean Islands and the Americas.

Vasco da Gama led the first expedition to travel from Europe to India by sailing around Africa.

FINISH

Explorer Ferdinand Magellan is best known for being the first person to circumnavigate (travel around) the globe.

ELIZABETHAN BRITAIN

Taking place from 1558-1603, the Elizabethan era is considered to be one of the greatest periods of British history.

During the reign of Queen Elizabeth I, England enjoyed much prosperity, works of great art, and exploration.

STEP INTO THE COURT OF QUEEN ELIZABETH THE FIRST AND AN AUDIENCE WITH HER MAJESTY!

START

Sir Francis Drake was the first Englishman to sail around the world and helped his country defeat the Spanish Armada in 1588.

Elizabeth I was the daughter of King Henry VIII and Anne Boleyn. She never married.

FINISH

During Queen Elizabeth's reign, William Shakespeare wrote many famous plays that were performed at the famous Globe Theatre in London.

AGE OF SCIENCE

The period between the fifteenth and eighteenth centuries was a time of great scientific discovery and invention.

Nicolaus Copernicus was a famous astronomer who discovered that the planets in our solar system orbit the Sun.

Galileo Galilei designed and created his own telescope, allowing him to discover the four largest moons of Jupiter!

START

FOLLOW GALILEO'S VIEWPOINT AND FIND THE CORRECT PATH THROUGH THE STAR CONSTELLATIONS.

Sir Isaac Newton developed the theory of gravity, the laws of motion, and a new type of mathematics called calculus!

German astronomer Johannes Kepler discovered that the planets in our solar system have oval-shaped orbits.

AGE OF EMPIRES

This map shows some of the world's largest empires at the times of their greatest size.

The British Empire was the largest in the world and at one point included North America, parts of Africa, and India.

The Spanish Empire conquered the Aztecs, Inca and Maya people, and also parts of Asia and Africa.

EMPIRE KEY

- French Empire (19th century)
- British Empire (early 20th century)
- Spanish Empire (mid 18th century)
- Ottoman Empire (17th century)

START

EXPLORE THE MAP OF EMPIRES AS YOU MAKE YOUR WAY AROUND THE GLOBE.

The Ottoman Empire was founded in Turkey and its conquests included Egypt, Greece, and Hungary.

In the seventeenth and eighteenth centuries the French Empire gained and lost large territories in North America and India.

MIGHTY RUSSIA

The Russian Empire was the third largest in history, at one point stretching across Europe, Asia, and Alaska in North America.

In the 1547, Ivan the Terrible became Russia's first tsar, or Russian emperor. He expanded Russia's empire into Siberia.

In 1922, multiple countries and territories formed the USSR (Union of Soviet Socialist Republics), also known as the Soviet Union.

GUIDE THE RUSSIAN VILLAGER THROUGH THE SNOW-COVERED ST. BASIL'S CATHEDRAL MAZE!

START

Feodor III was succeeded by Peter the Great, who became tsar of Russia and ruled jointly with Tsar Ivan V until 1696.

Empress Catherine the Great reigned from 1762–1796. She continued to expand and modernize the empire.

FINISH

FEUDAL JAPAN

During the Edo Period in Japan (1603-1868), the country was ruled by the emperor and his armies of samurai.

Japanese women wore garments called kimonos that were made of fine silk, and jade hair ornaments.

WHICH ROUTE SHOULD THE SAMURAI TAKE THROUGH THE GARDEN TO REACH THE PAGODA?

START

Samurai were soldiers who wore special protective clothing made from iron and leather. They followed a set of rules called Bushido or "way of the warrior."

Pagodas are unique
buildings that are
usually used as
Buddhist temples.
There are thousands
of pagodas in Japan.

FINISH

Kabuki is a
traditional Japanese
drama performed on
stage by actors in
elaborate makeup
and costumes.

INDUSTRIAL REVOLUTION

The eighteenth century in Great Britain was a time of technological innovation and the start of the Industrial Revolution.

During this period, many new ideas and inventions emerged that changed the world, making it seem like a much smaller place.

LEAD THE WORKER THROUGH THE BUSY FACTORY TO REACH THE SPINNING MACHINE AT THE END.

START

The first photograph was taken in 1826 by Joseph Nicéphore Niépce using a process called heliography.

The creation of the spinning jenny and power loom allowed for textiles and clothes to be mass-produced.

FINISH

The steam engine first appeared and soon became the main source of power for both manufacturing machines and transportation in steam locomotives.

AMERICAN REVOLUTION

Led by George Washington, American forces battled British troops for independence from 1775-1783.

George Washington was the first president of the United States and commander in chief during the Revolutionary War.

START

HELP THE AMERICAN SOLDIER REACH THE FRONT LINE TO BATTLE THE ADVANCING BRITISH TROOPS!

At the Battle of Saratoga, American forces managed to defeat the British, with heavy losses on both sides.

The Treaty of Paris
was signed on behalf
of King George III in
1783, acknowledging
the new nation of
the United States
of America.

Following the war,
the country created
the Constitution of
the United States
to guide the future
of the nation.

FINISH

AMERICAN EXPANSION

In 1803, US President Thomas Jefferson asked explorers Meriwether Lewis and William Clark to map the uncharted west of North America.

Lewis and Clark set out from St. Louis in 1804 with a team of around 40 men and made their way up the Missouri River.

They met many Native American tribes on their journey. A member of the Shoshone tribe, Sacagawea, helped the explorers by acting as a translator.

START

FOLLOW IN THE FOOTSTEPS OF LEWIS AND CLARK AS THEY EXPLORE THE UNCHARTED PACIFIC MIDWEST.

FINISH

They reached the
Pacific Ocean in 1805
and stayed over the
winter. The total journey
was more than
12,874 km (8,000 mi).

Lewis and Clark
encountered many
animals along the
way, including
grizzly bears
and prairie dogs!

FRENCH REVOLUTION

There was a time of huge change in France between 1789-1799 as people overthrew the monarchy.

The people wanted France's Louis XVI to give them certain rights. He refused and so was beheaded.

The French Revolution began when revolutionaries stormed an old prison and royal fortress called the Bastille.

LEAD THE REVOLUTIONARY THROUGH THE BATTLE-FILLED FRENCH STREET TO REACH THE BASTILLE.

START

The revolutionaries declared France a republic. It was now a country for the people and ruled by the people.

FINISH

The darkest period of the revolution came when a man called Robespierre executed people accused of treason.

71

NAPOLEON BONAPARTE

A brilliant military commander, Napoleon was also Emperor of the French and conquered much of Europe.

START

QUICKLY GUIDE THE FRENCH SOLDIER THROUGH THE HECTIC BATTLE TO REACH NAPOLEON BONAPARTE!

Napoleon was given command of the French army in Italy in 1796. He organized the troops and became a national hero.

In 1799, Napoleon returned to Paris and declared himself First Consul, a position that made him dictator of France.

Napoleon successfully conquered many European countries, including Spain, Italy, and Germany.

FINISH

Napoleon led French forces against the British at the Battle of Waterloo in 1815 and lost to the Duke of Wellington.

VICTORIAN BRITAIN

The Victorian era was a period of scientific inventions and technological advances.

Queen Victoria ruled Great Britain and Ireland for 63 years. During her reign, Britain became the largest empire that had ever existed.

Queen Victoria and her husband, Prince Albert encouraged developments in the arts, literature, and science.

HELP THE VICTORIAN NEWSPAPER SELLER GET TO THE OTHER SIDE OF TOWER BRIDGE!

START

The Great Exhibition was an international exhibition of culture and industry that took place in Hyde Park, London in 1851. It attracted visitors from all over the world.

Music halls, museums, and the popular novels of Charles Dickens helped keep the Victorians entertained.

FINISH

A boom in industry and factories during this time saw many cities, such as London, become overcrowded and dirty.

AGE OF INVENTION

The birth of the twentieth century saw the development of many new inventions that would change the world.

NAVIGATE THE WRIGHT BROTHERS' PLANE THROUGH THE MAZE TO THE LANDING STRIP.

START

In 1903, the Wright Brothers, Orville and Wilbur, flew the first powered plane at Kitty Hawk, N.C., USA.

In 1903, industrialist Henry Ford founded the Ford Motor Company and developed the assembly line for mass car production.

Ernest Rutherford was a brilliant New Zealand physicist and the first person to discover the structure of the atom.

One of the greatest physicists of all time, Albert Einstein released his paper on the theory of relativity in 1905.

$E = MC^2$

FINISH

WORLD WAR I

The first global war lasted from 1914-1918. Most of the fighting took place in Europe and over 10 million people died.

Devastating technological advances were made during the war, including the first tanks and fighter planes.

LEAD THE MEDIC THROUGH THE MUDDY TRENCHES OF WORLD I WAR TO REACH THE WOUNDED SOLDIERS.

START

The assassination of Archduke Franz Ferdinand in 1914 started a series of events that plunged the world into war.

There were three
Battles of Ypres,
with poison gas
being used by
Germany for the
first time in 1915.

The Battle of the
Somme in 1916 saw
massive casualties on
both sides with over
one million injured
or killed.

FINISH

THE GREAT DEPRESSION

In 1929, the US stock market collapsed, causing an economic global crisis that plunged much of the world into poverty.

FIND YOUR WAY THROUGH THE QUEUE OF PEOPLE TO BE SERVED AT THE SOUP KITCHEN.

As the Great Depression tightened its grip, many people found themselves out of work, homeless, and hungry.

START

The early twentieth century saw exciting forms of music enter mainstream US culture with the sounds of jazz and the blues.

Amelia Earhart was the first woman to fly solo across the Atlantic. She disappeared in 1937 while trying to fly around the world.

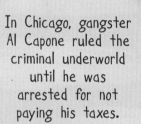

In Chicago, gangster Al Capone ruled the criminal underworld until he was arrested for not paying his taxes.

FINISH

WORLD WAR II

In 1939, a second global war broke out that would last for six years and result in over 70 million deaths.

The war began in Europe when the German leader, Adolf Hitler, ordered his army to invade Poland.

World War II was fought between the Axis and the Allies. The major Axis powers were Germany, Italy, and Japan. The major Allied powers were Britain, USA, the Soviet Union, and France.

START

CAREFULLY WORK YOUR WAY THROUGH THE BEACH LANDING ZONE TO SAFELY MAKE IT TO THE CLIFF BUNKER.

On June 6, 1944, the Allies started to take back Europe with over 150,000 troops during D-Day.

Many major battles took place around the world at El Alamein, Stalingrad, Midway, and Monte Cassino.

FINISH

THE COLD WAR

Following the end of World War II there was much distrust between the United States and the USSR.

During the Cold War, the USSR was led by Joseph Stalin, who would remain in power until 1953.

In 1961, the Communist government of East Berlin built a large wall separating the East and West of the city.

FOLLOW THE PATH OF THE BERLIN WALL AS IT SNAKES ITS WAY THROUGH EAST AND WEST BERLIN.

START

In 1957, the USSR successfully launched the first artificial satellite into space. It was called *Sputnik I*.

FINISH

In the US there was a huge boom in youth culture with the rise of rock 'n' roll artists such as Elvis Presley.

RIGHTS FOR ALL

The 1960s was a time of great change in the US, as the Civil Rights Movement pushed for equality for all Americans.

MAKE YOUR WAY THROUGH THE CROWD OF PEOPLE TO THE FRONT TO HEAR MARTIN LUTHER KING, JR.'S SPEECH.

START

During the 1960s, many American people protested the Vietnam War and refused to be drafted into the army.

In 1963, civil rights leader Martin Luther King, Jr. made his historic "I Have a Dream" speech to over 250,000 people.

John F. Kennedy was the youngest man ever to be elected president. He was assassinated in 1963 in Dallas, Texas.

In 1955, African-American Rosa Parks refused to give up her seat to a white man on a segregated bus, drawing attention to civil rights issues.

FINISH

THE SPACE RACE

During the Cold War, the United States and the Soviet Union started a race to see who had the best space technology.

Apollo 11 was launched into space in 1969, carrying three US astronauts on a three-day trip to the Moon.

On July 20, 1969, Neil Armstrong became the first person to walk on the surface of the Moon.

START

HELP GUIDE THE ASTRONAUT OVER THE SURFACE OF THE MOON TO REACH THE LUNAR LANDER!

In 1961, Soviet
cosmonaut Yuri
Gagarin became
the first human
being to orbit the
Earth in *Vostok I*.

FINISH

In total, six missions
landed humans on the
Moon. The last took
place in 1972 and
lasted for 12 days.

TIME OF CHANGE

As the world approached the end of the twentieth century, there were many important stories making the news in Russia.

NAVIGATE YOUR WAY THROUGH THE HISTORICAL EVENTS THAT TOOK PLACE IN EUROPE IN THE LATE TWENTIETH CENTURY!

START

Soviet leader Mikhail Gorbachev introduced "liberal" reforms, but it was too little too late.

The Berlin Wall was torn down in 1989, making way for a unified Berlin and Germany, and the creation of modern Russia.

The USSR started to collapse in the late 1980s and broke up into 15 independent states in 1991.

Countries once under the control of the USSR re-emerged, including Estonia, Kazakhstan, Moldova, and Ukraine.

FINISH

A NEW MILLENNIUM

As the planet entered a new century, all sorts of incredible technological breakthroughs have happened.

The World Wide Web was created in 1989 by Sir Timothy Berners-Lee as a global communication network.

Mobile phones were bulky and heavy when first invented. Modern cell phones have touchscreens and are super fast!

START

EXPLORE THE DIGITAL WORLD OF THE TWENTY-FIRST CENTURY AS HUMANITY BEGINS ITS NEXT 100 YEARS ON THE PLANET!

Online social media became very popular in the early 2000s with the release of platforms such as Facebook and Twitter.

The first video to be viewed on YouTube over a billion times was *Gangnam Style*, the 2012 music megahit from Psy!

a
b
c

FINISH

ANSWERS

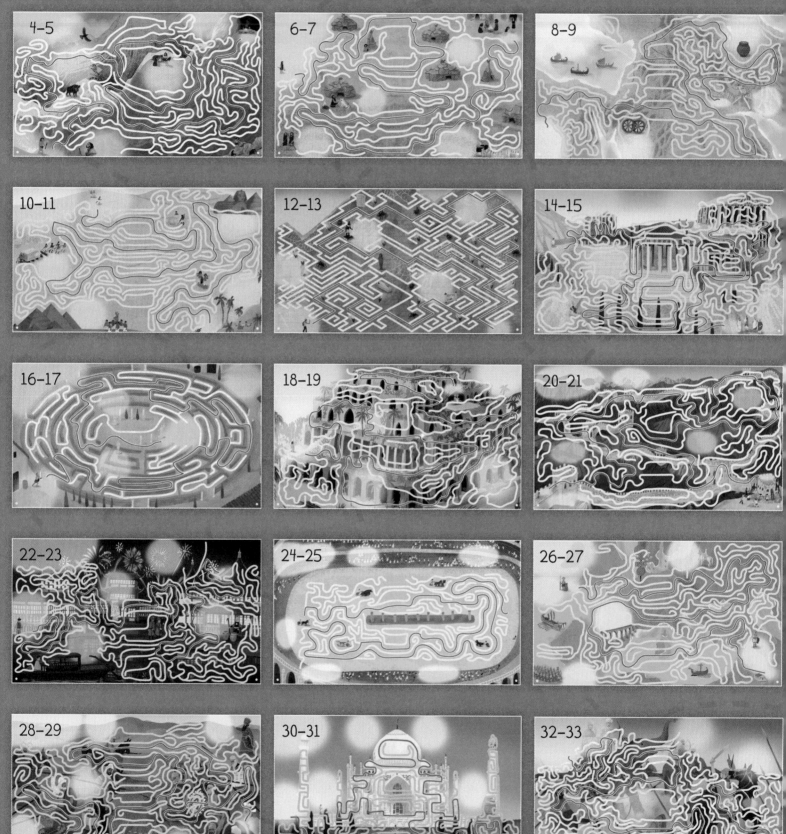